VIRAT KOHLI

INDIAN CRICKETER

MR VIVEK KUMAR PANDEY SHAMBHUNATH

Copyright © Mr Vivek Kumar Pandey Shambhunath
All Rights Reserved.

ISBN 979-888530988-2

This book has been published with all efforts taken to make the material error-free after the consent of the author. However, the author and the publisher do not assume and hereby disclaim any liability to any party for any loss, damage, or disruption caused by errors or omissions, whether such errors or omissions result from negligence, accident, or any other cause.

While every effort has been made to avoid any mistake or omission, this publication is being sold on the condition and understanding that neither the author nor the publishers or printers would be liable in any manner to any person by reason of any mistake or omission in this publication or for any action taken or omitted to be taken or advice rendered or accepted on the basis of this work. For any defect in printing or binding the publishers will be liable only to replace the defective copy by another copy of this work then available.

Short biography of Virat Kohli and about life.During writing this book no character & no religious are harmed written by Mr Vivek Kumar Pandey. winner youngest writer award 1st rank in india 2020.He is only one writer can publish 700+ own book that was greatest successfull in his life .

Contents

Foreword

Author biography in English :MY NAME IS VIVEK KUMAR PANDEY . I WAS BORN IN 30 SEP 2002,I AM FROM SURAT GUJARAT INDIA.MY DREAM WAS TO BE GOOD WRITERS ,MY FAMILY SUPPORTED ME TO SUCCESSFUL AND I CAN DO IT MY SELF.How do I write? That is a question, I believe, that cannot be honestly answered by me."CELEBRATING YOUNGEST WRITER AWARD WINNER IN GUJARAT 1ST RANK" MR PANDEY JI . I may think I did a good job writing something when in reality it could be horrible. The reader is the one who decides the quality of my writing. I do not find writing to be natural to me and therefore find it to be a real challenge. My trick as a challenged writer is to do the best I can and know that I am happy with the final outcome. It may take a while to do my best and there may be quite a few problems I run into along the way.

I am not a greedy person those who are thinking about me and my self I never tried it anyone people suffering from sadness ,I trying to get promoted people suffering from happiness and joy in your Life Time. Now in current situation in India and also world people are unemployed and have no many but our indian governor help to people to get free food from ration card , i also take part in leadership team ,i am Motivational speaker , Film script writer. There was my two dream firstly writer and secondly actor & also my own film is upcoming soon i done almost completely completed script for my film .I AM GOING TO SAY WORD OF HEART TOUCH OUT PLEASE READ IT" , firstly i thanks my father he supports me in this field they always getting inspired me by own his words and behavior ,they always said that he was a biggest person in the world in future and also they purchase fruit and chocolate for me in anytime & anyway , firstly my father buy him then call me Vivek you want a chocolate i will say yes papa but how many tell me ,papa: you tell me how much i buy him i told 1 or 2 chocolate but my father purchase whole the boxes of chocolate and they get suprised me. MY FATHER WAS BORN IN " 20 SEPTEMBER" 1971 IN INDIA.

1) MY FATHER FAVORITE CLOTHES IS KURTA PAIJMA AND ALSO STYLES SHOE

2) FAVORITE SINGER IS KISHORE DA

3) FAVORITE STATE GUJARAT AND KOLKATA , HIS VILLAGE IN BIHAR

4) FAVORITE COLOR BLACK AND WHITE

THEY ALSO LOVE cricket like IPL and one day t-20 .they also like watching a News daily and heard the song daily ,they also interested in tik tok video but in current time tik tok is banned in india but also few videos are in you tube. In lockdown time my family and me very enjoy day daily. my father play daily ludo with his sister and son, daughter.they always loved tea and coffee anytime call me "। वविक थोडा़ चाय बनाओना वविक तुम्हारे हाथ का चाय अच्छा लगता है". I make it tea for my father but some reason after the April to june they are suffering from fever and cough , weakness on 6 June 2020 my father death. they not told me say bye bye his life. After death of 6 June on 10 june my mom and dad anniversary.but my father is Best in the world they can do anything for me please take care of father and respect it of your parents.

CHAPTER ONE

Virat Kohli

- Virat Kohli

1. During writing this book no character & no religious are harmed written by Mr Vivek Kumar Pandey.

Virat Kohli born 5 November 1988 is an Indian cricketer and the captain of India national cricket team in Tests. He plays for Delhi in domestic cricket and Royal Challengers Bangalore in the Indian Premier League as a right-handed batsman. Kohli is often considered as one of the best cricket player in the world and widely regarded as one of the greatest cricket players of all time.

Kohli made his Test debut in 2011. He reached the number one spot in the ICC rankings for ODI batsmen for the first time in 2013. He has won Man of the Tournament twice at the ICC World Twenty20 (in 2014 and 2016). He also holds the world record of being the fastest to 23,000 international runs.

Kohli has been the recipient of many awards– most notably the Sir Garfield Sobers Trophy (ICC Men's Cricketer of the Decade): 2011–2020; Sir Garfield Sobers Trophy (ICC Cricketer of the Year) in 2017 and 2018; ICC Test Player of the Year (2018); ICC ODI Player of the Year (2012, 2017, 2018) and Wisden Leading Cricketer in the World (2016, 2017 and 2018). At the national level, he was awarded the Arjuna Award in 2013, the Padma Shri under the sports category in 2017 and the Rajiv Gandhi Khel Ratna award, the highest sporting honour in India, in 2018. He is ranked as one of the world's most famous athletes by ESPN and one of the most valuable athlete brands by Forbes. In 2018, Time magazine named him one of the 100 most influential people in the world. In 2020, he was ranked 66th in

Forbes list of the top 100 highest-paid athletes in the world for the year 2020 with estimated earnings of over $26 million.

- *Early life*

Virat Kohli was born on 5 November 1988 in Delhi into a Punjabi Hindu family.His father, Prem Kohli, worked as a criminal lawyer and his mother, Saroj Kohli, is a housewife.He has an older brother, Vikash, and an older sister, Bhavna.

Kohli was raised in Uttam Nagar and started his schooling at Vishal Bharti Public School. In 1998, the West Delhi Cricket Academy was created and a nine-year-old Kohli was part of its first intake. Kohli trained at the academy under Rajkumar Sharma and also played matches at the Sumeet Dogra Academy at Vasundhara Enclave at the same time. In ninth grade, he shifted to Saviour Convent in Paschim Vihar to help his cricket practice.Kohli's family lived in Meera Bagh until 2015 when they moved to Gurgaon.Kohli's father died on 18 December 2006 due to a stroke after being bed-ridden for a month.

- *Youth and domestic career*

- Kohli at post match event, India vs Newzealand, 2010 Delhi

Kohli first played for Delhi Under-15 team in October 2002 in the 2002–03 Polly Umrigar Trophy. He became the captain of the team for the 2003–04 Polly Umrigar Trophy. In late 2004, he was selected in the Delhi Under-17 team for the 2003–04 Vijay Merchant Trophy. Delhi Under-17s won the 2004–05 Vijay Merchant Trophy in which Kohli finished as the highest run-scorer with 757 runs from 7 matches at an average of 84.11 with two centuries.In February 2006, he made his List A debut for Delhi against Services but did not get to bat.

Kohli made his first-class debut for Delhi against Tamil Nadu in November 2006, at the age of 18, he scored 10 runs in his debut innings. He came into the spotlight in December when he decided to play for his team against Karnataka on the day after his father's death and went on to score 90. He went directly to the funeral after he got out in the match. He scored a total of 257 runs from 6 matches at an average of 36.71 in that season.

- *India Under-19*

In July 2006, Kohli was selected in the India Under-19 squad on its tour of England. He averaged 105 in the three-match ODI series against England Under-19s and 49 in the three-match Test series. India Under-19 went on to win both the series. In September, the India Under-19 team toured Pakistan. Kohli averaged 58 in the Test series and 41.66 in the ODI series against Pakistan Under-19s.

In April 2007, he made his Twenty20 debut and finished as the highest run-getter for his team in the Inter-State T20 Championship with 179 runs at an average of 35.80. In July–August 2007, the India Under-19 team toured Sri Lanka. In the triangular series against Sri Lanka Under-19s and Bangladesh Under-19s, Kohli was the second highest run-getter with 146 runs at an average of 29 from 5 matches. In the two-match Test series that followed, he scored 244 runs at an average of 122 including a century and a fifty.

In February–March 2008, Kohli captained the victorious Indian team at the 2008 Under-19 Cricket World Cup held in Malaysia. Batting at number 3, he scored 235 runs in 6 matches at an average of 47 and finished as the tournament's third-highest run-getter and one of the three batsmen to score a hundred in the tournament. He was instrumental in India's three-wicket semi-final win over New Zealand Under-19s in which he took 2 wickets and scored 43 in the tense run-chase and was awarded the man of the match.

- *IPL*

Following the Under-19 World Cup, Kohli was bought by the Indian Premier League franchise Royal Challengers Bangalore for $30,000 on a youth contract. In June 2008, Kohli and his Under-19 teammates Pradeep Sangwan and Tanmay Srivastava were awarded the Border-Gavaskar scholarship. The scholarship allowed the three players to train for six weeks at Cricket Australia's Centre of Excellence in Brisbane. He was also picked in the India Emerging Players squad for the four-team Emerging Players Tournament and scored 206 runs in six matches at an average of 41.20.

- *International career*

- Early years

In August 2008, Kohli was included in the Indian ODI squad for tour of Sri Lanka and the Champions Trophy in Pakistan. Prior to the Sri Lankan tour, Kohli had played only eight List A matches. So, his selection was called a "surprise call-up". During the Sri Lankan tour, as both first-choice openers Sachin Tendulkar and Virender Sehwag were injured, Kohli batted as a makeshift opener throughout the series.He made his international debut, at the age of 19, in the first ODI of the tour and was dismissed for 12. He made his first ODI half century, a score of 54, in the fourth match.He had scores of 37, 25 and 31 in the other three matches. India won the series 3–2 which was India's first ODI series win against Sri Lanka in Sri Lanka.

After the postponement of Champions Trophy to 2009, Kohli was picked as a replacement for the injured Shikhar Dhawan in the India A squad for the unofficial Tests against Australia A in September 2008. He batted only once in the two-match series, and scored 49 in that innings.Later that month in September 2008, he played for Delhi in the Nissar Trophy against SNGPL (winners of Quaid-i-Azam Trophy from Pakistan) and top-scored for Delhi in both innings, with 52 and 197. The match was drawn but SNGPL won the trophy on first-innings lead. In October 2008, Kohli played for Indian Board President's XI in a four-day tour match against Australia.

Kohli, after recovering from a minor shoulder injury, returned to the national team replacing the injured Gautam Gambhir in the Indian squad for the tri-series in Sri Lanka. He batted at number 4 for India in the 2009 ICC Champions Trophy because of an injury to Yuvraj Singh. In the group match against the West Indies, Kohli scored an unbeaten 79 in India's successful chase of 130 and was awarded man of the match award. Kohli played as a reserve batsman in the seven-match home ODI series against Australia, appearing in two matches.

He found a place in the home ODI series against Sri Lanka in December 2009 and scored 27 and 54 in the first two ODIs before making way for Yuvraj who regained fitness for the third ODI. However, Yuvraj's finger injury recurred leading to him being ruled out indefinitely. Kohli returned to the team in the fourth ODI at Kolkata and scored his first ODI century–107 off 114 balls–sharing a 224-run partnership for the third wicket with Gambhir, who made his personal best score of 150. India won by seven wickets to seal the series 3–1. The man of the match was awarded to Gambhir who gave the award to Kohli.

Tendulkar was rested for the tri-nation ODI tournament in Bangladesh in January 2010, which enabled Kohli to play in each of India's five matches.

Against Bangladesh, he scored 91 to help secure a win after India collapsed to 51/3 early in their run-chase of 297. In the next match against Sri Lanka, Kohli ended unbeaten on 71 to help India win the match with a bonus point having chased down their target of 214 within 33 overs. The next day, he scored his second ODI century, against Bangladesh, bringing up the mark with the winning runs.He became only the third Indian batsman to score two ODI centuries before their 22nd birthday, after Tendulkar and Suresh Raina. Kohli was much praised for his performances during the series in particular by the Indian captain Dhoni. Although Kohli made only two runs in the final against Sri Lanka in a four-wicket Indian defeat, he finished as the leading run-getter of the series with 275 runs from five innings at an average of 91.66. In the three-match ODI series at home against South Africa in February, Kohli batted in two games and had scores of 31 and 57.

- *Rise through the ranks*

Raina was named captain and Kohli vice-captain for the tri-series against Sri Lanka and Zimbabwe in Zimbabwe in May–June 2010, as many first-choice players skipped the tour. Kohli made 168 runs at an average of 42.00 including two fifties,but India suffered three defeats in four matches and crashed out of the series. During the series, Kohli became the fastest Indian batsman to reach 1,000 runs in ODI cricket.He made his T20I debut against Zimbabwe at Harare and scored an unbeaten 26. Later that month, Kohli batted at 3 in an Indian team throughout the 2010 Asia Cup and scored a total of 67 runs at an average of 16.75. His struggles with form continued in the tri-series against Sri Lanka and New Zealand in Sri Lanka where he averaged 15.

- *Kohli batting in an ODI against New Zealand in December 2010*

Despite the poor run of form, Kohli was retained in the ODI squad for a three-match series against Australia in October, and in the only completed match of the series at Visakhapatnam, scored his third ODI century–118 off 121 balls–which helped India reach the target of 290 after losing the openers early.Winning the man of the match, he admitted that he was under pressure to keep his place in the team after failures in the two previous series. Part of a largely inexperienced teamfor the home ODI series against New Zealand, Kohli scored a match-winning 104-ball 105, his fourth ODI hundred and second in succession, in the first game, and followed it up with 64 and 63* in the next two matches.India completed a 5–0 whitewash of New Zealand, while Kohli's performance in the series helped him become a regular in the ODI team and made him a strong contender for a spot in India's World Cup squad. He was India's leading run-scorer in ODIs in 2010, with 995 runs from 25 matches at an average of 47.38 including three centuries and seven fifties.

Kohli was India's leading run-getter in the five-match ODI series of the South African tour in January 2011, with 193 runs at an average of 48.25 including two fifties, both in Indian defeats. During the series, he jumped to number two spot on the ICC Rankings for ODI batsmen,and was named in India's 15-man squad for the World Cup. The inclusion of both Kohli and Raina in the World Cup squad resulted in speculations about which of the two batsmen will make it to the playing eleven. Days before India's first match of the tournament, Indian captain Dhoni indicated that the in-form Kohli is likely to be preferred over Raina.

Kohli played in every match of India's successful World Cup campaign. He scored an unbeaten 100, his fifth ODI century, in the first match against Bangladesh and became the first Indian batsman to score a century on World Cup debut.In the next four group matches he had low scores of 8, 34, 12 and 1 against England, Ireland, Netherlands and South Africa respectively. Having returned to form with 59 against the West Indies, he scored only 24 and 9 in the quarter-final against Australia and semi-final against Pakistan respectively.[48] In the final against Sri Lanka at Mumbai, he scored 35, sharing an 83-run partnership with Gambhir for the third wicket after India had lost both openers within the seventh over chasing 275. This partnership is regarded as "one of the turning points in the match", as India went on to win the match by six wickets and lift the World Cup for the first time since 1983.

- *Consistent performance in limited overs*

- Kohli fielding during a match in December 2010

When India toured the West Indies in June–July 2011, they selected a largely inexperienced squad, resting Tendulkar and others such as- Gambhir and Sehwag missing out due to injuries. Kohli was one of three uncapped players in the Test squad. He found success in the ODI series which India won 3–2, with a total of 199 runs at an average of 39.80. His best efforts came in the second ODI at Port of Spain where he won the man of the match for his score of 81 which gave India a seven-wicket victory, and the fifth ODI at Kingston where his innings of 94 came in a seven-wicket defeat. Kohli made his Test debut at Kingston in the first match of the Test series that followed. He batted at 5 and was dismissed for 4 and 15 caught behind by Fidel Edwards in both innings.India went on to win the Test series 1–0 but Kohli amassed just 76 runs from five innings, struggling against the short ball and was particularly troubled by the fast bowling of Edwards, who dismissed him three times in the series.

Initially dropped from the Test squad for India's four-match series in England in July and August due to poor performance in his debut series, Kohli was recalled as a replacement for the injured Yuvraj,though did not play in any match in the series. He found moderate success in the subsequent ODI series in which he averaged 38.80. His score of 55 in the first ODI at Chester-le-Street was followed by a string of low scores in the next three matches. In the last game of the series, Kohli scored his sixth ODI hundred–107 runs off 93 balls–and shared a 170-run third-wicket partnership with Rahul Dravid, who was playing his last ODI, to help India post their first 300-plus total of the tour. Kohli was dismissed hit wicket in that innings which was the only century in the series by any player on either team and earned him praise for his "hard work" and "maturity". However, England won the match by D/L method and the series 3–0.

In October 2011, Kohli was the leading run-scorer of the five-match home ODI series against England which India won 5–0. He scored a total of 270 runs across five matches at an average of 90, including unbeaten knocks of 112 from 98 balls at Delhi, where he put on an unbroken 209-run partnership with Gambhir, and 86 at Mumbai, both in successful run-chases. Owing to his ODI success, Kohli was included, ahead of Raina, in the Test squad to face the West Indies in November. In competition with Yuvraj Singh for the number six position, it was not until the final match of the series that Kohli was selected in the team. He scored a pair of fifties in the match, with his first innings score of 52 ensuring India avoided follow-on. India won the subsequent ODI series 4–1 in which Kohli managed to accumulate 243 runs at 60.75.

During the series, Kohli scored his eighth ODI century and his second at Visakhapatnam, where he made 117 off 123 balls in India's run-chase of 270, a knock which raised his reputation as "an expert of the chase". Kohli ended up as the leading run-getter in ODIs for the year 2011, with 1381 runs from 34 matches at 47.62 including four centuries and eight fifties.

- *Ascension to ODI vice-captaincy*

Having found a place in India's Test squad for the tour of Australia in December 2011, Kohli top-scored with 132 in a tour match against Cricket Australia Chairman's XI to strengthen his case for a spot in the playing eleven ahead of Rohit Sharma. Kohli failed to go past 25 in the first two Tests, as his defensive technique was exposed.While fielding on the boundary during the second day of the second match, he gestured to the crowd with his middle finger for which he was fined 50% of his match fee by the match referee.He top-scored in each of India's innings in the third Test at Perth, with 44 and 75, even as India surrendered to their second consecutive innings defeat. In the fourth and final match at Adelaide, Kohli scored his maiden Test century of 116 runs in the first innings; it was the only century scored by an Indian in the series. India suffered a 0–4 whitewash and Kohli, India's top run-scorer in the series, was described as "the lone bright spot in an otherwise nightmare visit for the tourists".

- *Kohli fielding during a CB Series match against Australia in February 2012*

In the first seven matches of the Commonwealth Bank triangular series that India played against hosts Australia and Sri Lanka, Kohli made two fifties–77 at Perth and 66 at Brisbane–both against Sri Lanka. India registered two wins, a tie and four losses in these seven matches, which meant that they needed a bonus point win their last group match against Sri Lanka at Hobart, to stay in contention for qualifying for the finals series. Being set a target of 321 by Sri Lanka, Kohli came to the crease with India's score at 86/2 and went on to score 133 not out from 86 balls to take India to a comfortable win with 13 overs to spare. India earned a bonus point with the win and Kohli was named Man of the Match for his knock, which included scoring 24 runs in an over by Lasith Malinga. Former Australian cricketer and commentator Dean Jones rated Kohli's innings as "one of the greatest ODI knocks of all time". However, Sri Lanka beat Australia three days later in their last group fixture and knocked India out of the series. With 373 runs at 53.28, Kohli once again finished as India's highest run-scorer and lone centurion of the series.

Kohli was appointed the vice-captain for the 2012 Asia Cup in Bangladesh on the back of his fine performance in Australia. Kohli was in fine form during the tournament, finishing as the leading run-scorer with 357 runs at an average of 119.He scored 108 in the first match against Sri Lanka in a 50-run Indian victory, while India lost their next match to Bangladesh in which he made 66. In the final group stage match against Pakistan, he scored a personal best 183 off 148 balls, his 11th ODI century. Coming in at 0/1, he struck 22 fours and a six in his innings to help India to chase down 330, their highest successful ODI run-chase at the time. His knock was the highest individual score in Asia Cup history surpassing previous record of 144 by Younis Khan in 2004, the joint-second highest score, with Dhoni, in an ODI run-chase and the highest individual score against Pakistan in ODIs surpassing previous record of 156 by Brian Lara in 2005. Kohli was awarded the man of the match in both the matches that India won,but India could not progress to the final of the tournament.

In July–August 2012, Kohli struck two centuries in the five-match ODI tour of Sri Lanka–106 off 113 balls at Hambantota and 128* off 119 balls at Colombo–winning man of the match in both games.India won the series 4–1 and on the account of scoring the most runs in the series, Kohli was named player of the series. In the one-off T20I that followed, he scored a 48-ball 68, his first T20I fifty, and won the player of the series award. Kohli scored his second Test century at Bangalore during New Zealand's tour of India and won man of the match award. India won the two-match series 2–0, and Kohli averaged 106 with one hundred and two fifties from three innings. In the subsequent T20I series, he scored 70 runs off 41 balls, but India lost the match by one run and the series 1–0. He continued to be in good form during the 2012 ICC World Twenty20 in Sri Lanka, with 185 runs, the highest among Indian batsmen, from 5 matches at an average of 46.25. He hit two fifties during the tournament, 50 against Afghanistan in the group stageand 78* against Pakistan in the Super Eights, winning man of the match for both innings. He was named in the ICC 'Team of the Tournament'.

Kohli's Test form dipped during the first three matches of England's tour of India, between October 2012 and January 2013, with a top score of 20 and England leading the series 2–1.He scored a patient 103 from 295 balls in the last match on a slow and low pitch at Nagpur, keeping India in contention of drawing the series. However, the match ended in a draw and

England won their first Test series in India in 28 years. Against Pakistan in December 2012, Kohli averaged 18 in the T20Is and 4.33 in the ODIs, being troubled by the fast bowlers, particularly Junaid Khan, who dismissed him on all three occasions in the ODI series. Kohli had a quiet ODI series against England, apart from a match-winning 77* in the third ODI at Ranchi, with a total of 155 runs at an average of 38.75.

Kohli scored his fourth Test century (107) at Chennai in the first match of the home Test series against Australia in February 2013.India completed a 4–0 series sweep, becoming the first team to whitewash Australia in more than four decades. Kohli averaged 56.80 in the series .

- *Kohli batting against South Africa in Cardiff during the Champions Trophy in June 2013*

In June 2013, Kohli featured in the ICC Champions Trophy in England which India won. He scored a match-winning 144 against Sri Lanka in a warm-up match. He scored 31, 22 and 22* in India's group matches against South Africa, West Indies and Pakistan respectively, while India qualified for the semi-finals with an undefeated record. In the semi-final against Sri Lanka at Cardiff, he struck 58* in an eight-wicket win for India. The final between India and England at Birmingham was reduced to 20 overs after a rain delay. India batted first and Kohli top-scored with 43 from 34 balls, sharing a sixth-wicket partnership of 47 runs off 33 balls with Ravindra Jadeja and helping India reach 129/7 in 20 overs. India went on to secure a five-run win and their second consecutive ICC ODI tournament victory. He was also named as part of the 'Team of the Tournament' by the ICC.

- *Setting records*

Kohli stood-in as the captain for the first ODI of the triangular series in the West Indies after Dhoni injured himself during the match. India lost the match by one wicket, and Dhoni was subsequently ruled out of the series with Kohli being named the captain for the remaining matches.In his second match as captain, Kohli scored his first century as captain, making 102 off 83 balls against the West Indies at Port of Spain in a bonus point win for India. Many senior players, including Dhoni, were rested for the five-match ODI tour of Zimbabwe in July 2013, with Kohli being appointed captain for an entire series for the first time. In the first game of the series at Harare, he struck 115 runs from 108 balls, helping India chase down the target of 229 and winning the man of the match award.He batted on two more occasions in the series in which he had scores of 14 and 68*. India completed a 5–0 sweep of the series; their first in an away ODI series.

Kohli had a successful time with the bat in the seven-match ODI series against Australia. After top-scoring with 61 in the opening loss at Pune, he struck the fastest century by an Indian in ODIs in the second match at Jaipur. Reaching the milestone in just 52 balls and putting up an unbroken 186-run second-wicket partnership with Rohit Sharma that came in 17.2 overs, Kohli's innings of 100* helped India chase down the target of 360 for the loss of one wicket with more than six overs to spare. This chase was the second-highest successful run-chase in ODI cricket at the time, while Kohli's knock became the fastest century against Australia and the third-fastest in a run-chase. He followed that innings with 68 in the next match at Mohali in another Indian defeat, before the next two matches were washed out by rain.

In the sixth ODI at Nagpur, he struck 115 off only 66 balls to help India successfully chase the target of 351 and level the series 2–2 and won the man of the match.He reached the 100-run mark in 61 balls, making it the third-fastest ODI century by an Indian batsman, and also became the fastest batsman in the world to score 17 hundreds in ODI cricket. India clinched the series after winning the last match in which he was run out for a duck. At the conclusion of the series, Kohli moved to the top position in the ICC ODI batsmen rankings for the first time in his career.

Kohli batted twice in the two-match Test series against the West Indies, and had scores of 3 and 57 being dismissed by Shane Shillingford in both innings. This was also the last Test series for Tendulkar and Kohli was expected to take Tendulkar's number 4 batting position after the series. In the first game of the three-match ODI series that followed at Kochi, Kohli made 86 to seal a six-wicket win and won the man of the match. During the match, he also equalled Viv Richards' record of becoming the fastest batsman to make 5,000 runs in ODI cricket, reaching the landmark in his 114th innings. He missed out on his third century at Visakhapatnam in the next match, after being dismissed for 99 playing a hook shot off Ravi Rampaul. India lost the match by two wickets, but took the series 2–1 after winning the last match at Kanpur. With 204 runs at 68.00, Kohli finished the series as the leading run-getter and was awarded the man of the series.

- *Overseas season*

Virat Kohli batting against UAE during 2015 Cricket World Cup

India toured South Africa in December 2013 for three ODIs and two Tests. Kohli averaged 15.50 in the ODIs, including a duck. In the first Test at Johannesburg, playing his first Test in South Africa and batting at 4 for the first time, Kohli scored 119 and 96. His hundred was the first by a subcontinent batsman at the venue since 1998. The match ended in a draw, and Kohli was awarded man of the match. India failed to win a single match on the tour, losing the second Test by 10 wickets in which he made 46 and 11.

- Kohli continued to amass runs on the subsequent New Zealand tour. He averaged 58.21 in the five-match ODI series in which his efforts of 111-ball 123 at Napier, 65-ball 78 at Hamilton and 78-ball 82 at Wellington all went in vain as India were defeated 4–0. He made 214 runs at 71.33 in the two-match Test series that followed including an unbeaten 105 on the last day of the second Test at Wellington that helped India save the match.

India then traveled to Bangladesh for the Asia Cup and World Twenty20. Dhoni was ruled out of the Asia Cup after suffering a side strain during the New Zealand tour, which led to Kohli being named the captain for the tournament. Kohli scored 136 off 122 balls in India's opening match against Bangladesh, sharing a 213-run third-wicket stand with Ajinkya Rahane, which helped India successfully chase 280.It was his 19th ODI century and his fifth in Bangladesh, making him the batsman with most ODI centuries in Bangladesh. India were knocked out of the tournament after narrow losses against Sri Lanka and Pakistan, in which Kohli scored 48 and 5 respectively.

- Dhoni returned from injury to captain the team for 2014 ICC World Twenty20 and Kohli was named vice-captain. In India's opening match of the tournament against Pakistan, Kohli top-scored with 36 not out to guide India to a seven-wicket win. He scored 54 off 41 balls in the next game against West Indies and an unbeaten 57 from 50 balls against Bangladesh, both in successful run-chases. In the semi-final, he made an unbeaten 72 in 44 deliveries to help India achieve the target of 173 with six wickets and five balls to spare. He won the man of the match for this knock. India posted 130/4 in the final against Sri Lanka, in which Kohli scored 77 from 58 balls, and eventually lost the match by six wickets. Kohli had made a total of 319 runs in the tournament at an average of 106.33, a record for most runs by an individual batsman in a single World Twenty20 tournament, for which he won the Man of the Tournament award.

Kohli and other senior players were rested for India's tour of Bangladesh ahead of the England tour. India conceded a 3–1 defeat in the five-match Test series against England despite leading it 1–0 after the first two Tests. Kohli fared poorly in the series averaging just 13.40 in 10 innings scoring 134 runs overall with a top score of 39.It was a nightmare tour for him as He was dismissed for single-digit scores on six occasions in the series and was particularly susceptible to the swinging ball on off stump line, being dismissed several times edging the ball to the wicket-keeper or slip fielders. Man of the series James Anderson got Kohli's wicket four times, while Kohli's batting technique was questioned by analysts and former cricketers. India won the ODI series that followed 3–1, but Kohli's struggles with the bat continued with an average of 18 in four innings. In the one-off T20I, he scored 41-ball 66, his first fifty-plus score of the tour on the last match of the tour. India lost the match by three runs, but Kohli reached the number one spot for T20I batsmen in the ICC rankings.

Kohli had a successful time during India's home ODI series win over the West Indies in October 2014. His 62 in the second ODI at Delhi was his first fifty across Tests and ODIs in 16 innings since February,and he stated that he got his "confidence back" with the innings.He struck his 20th ODI hundred–127 runs in 114 balls–in the fourth match at Dharamsala. India registered a 59-run victory and Kohli was awarded man of the match.

Dhoni was rested for the five-match ODI series against Sri Lanka in November, enabling Kohli to lead the team for another full series. Kohli batted at 4 throughout the series and made scores of 22, 49, 53 and 66 in the first four ODIs, with India leading the series 4–0. In the fifth ODI at Ranchi, Kohli came in to bat with India at 14/2 in pursuit of 287. He made an unbeaten 139 off 126 balls to give his team a three-wicket win and a whitewash of Sri Lanka. Kohli was awarded player of the series, and it was the second whitewash under his captaincy. During the series he became the fastest batsman in the world to go past the 6000-run mark in ODIs.With 1054 ODI runs at 58.55 in 2014, he became the second player in the world after Sourav Ganguly to make more than 1,000 runs in ODIs for four consecutive calendar years.

- *Test captaincy*

- Virat Kohli after scoring a hundred against England in 2018 Test series

For the first Test of the Australian tour in December 2014, Dhoni was not part of the Indian team at Adelaide due to an injury, and Kohli took the reins as Test captain for the first time. Kohli scored 115 in India's first innings, becoming the fourth Indian to score a hundred on Test captaincy debut. In their second innings, India were set a target of 364 to be scored on the fifth day. Kohli came in to bat when the Indian innings was reduced to 57/2 and started batting aggressively. He put on 185 runs for the third wicket with Murali Vijay before Vijay's dismissal, which triggered a batting collapse. From 242/2, India was bowled out for 315 with Kohli's 141 off 175 balls being the top score.

Dhoni returned to the team as captain for the second match at Brisbane where Kohli scored 19 and 1 in a four-wicket defeat for India.In the Melbourne Boxing Day Test, Kohli was India's top-scorer in both innings. He made his personal best Test score of 169 in the first innings while sharing a 262-run partnership with Rahane, India's biggest partnership outside Asia in ten years. Kohli followed it with a score of 54 in India's second innings on the fifth day, helping his team draw the Test match.Dhoni announced his retirement from Test cricket at the conclusion of this match, and Kohli was appointed as the full-time Test captain ahead of the fourth Test at Sydney. Captaining the Test team for the second time, Kohli hit 147 in the first innings of the match and became the first batsman in Test cricket history to score three hundreds in his first three innings as Test captain. He was dismissed for 46 in the second innings and India hung in for another draw.Kohli's total of 692 runs in four Tests was the most by any Indian batsman in a Test series in Australia.

In January 2015, India failed to win a single match in the tri-nation ODI series against the hosts Australia and England. Kohli was unable to replicate his Test success in ODIs, failing to make a two-digit score in any of the four games. Kohli's ODI form did not improve in the lead-up to the World Cup, with scores of 18 and 5 in the warm-up matches against Australia and Afghanistan respectively.

- *Kohli batting against the UAE in Perth during a group stage match of the 2015 World Cup*

In the first match of the World Cup against Pakistan at Adelaide, Kohli hit 107 in 126 balls, sharing 100-plus partnerships with both Dhawan and Raina, to help India set a total of 300 and win the match by 76 runs. For his knock, he was awarded the man of the match award, his 20th in ODIs and second in a World Cup match. Kohli also became first Indian batsman to score a century against Pakistan in a World Cup match. He was dismissed for 46 in India's second match against South Africa after another century partnership with opening batsman Dhawan. India went on to post 307 in 50 overs and register a 130-run victory in the match. India batted second in their remaining four group matches in which Kohli scored 33*, 33, 44* and 38 against UAE, West Indies, Ireland and Zimbabwe respectively. India went on to secure wins in these four fixtures and top the Pool B points with an undefeated record. In India's 109-run victory in the quarter-final over Bangladesh, Kohli was dismissed by Rubel Hossain for 3 edging the ball to the wicket-keeper. India was eliminated in the semi-final by Australia at Melbourne, where Kohli was dismissed for 1 off 13 balls, top-edging a short-pitched delivery from Mitchell Johnson.

Kohli had a slump in form when India toured Bangladesh in June 2015. He contributed only 14 in the one-off Test which ended in a draw and averaged 16.33 in the ODI series which Bangladesh won 2–1.Kohli ended his streak of low scores by scoring his 11th Test hundred in the first Test of the Sri Lankan tour which India lost. India came back and won the next two matches to seal the series 2–1, Kohli's first series win as Test captain and India's first away Test series win in four years.

During South Africa's tour of India, Kohli became the fastest batsman in the world to make 1,000 runs in T20I cricket, reaching the milestone in his 27th innings. In the ODI series, he made 77 at Rajkot and a match-winning 138 in the fourth ODI at Chennai that helped India draw level in the series. India lost the series after a defeat in the final ODI and Kohli finished the series with an average of 49. India came back to beat the top-ranked South African team 3–0 in the four-match Test series under Kohli's captaincy, and climbed to number two position on the ICC Test rankings. He scored a total of 200 runs in the series at 33.33, including 44 and 88 in the fourth match at Delhi.

- *Virat Kohli's record as captain*

Kohli started 2016 with scores of 91 and 59 in the first two ODIs of the limited-overs tour of Australia. He followed it up with a pair of hundreds–a run-a-ball 117 at Melbourne and 106 from 92 balls at Canberra–in the next two matches. During the course of the series, he became the fastest batsman in the world to cross the 7000-run mark in ODIs, getting to the milestone in his 161st innings, and the fastest to get to 25 centuries. After the ODI series ended in a 1–4 loss, the Indian team came back to whitewash the Australians 3–0 in the T20I series. Kohli made fifties in all three T20Is with scores of 90 not out, 59 not out and 50, winning two man of the matches as well as the man of the series award. He was also instrumental in India winning the Asia Cup in Bangladesh the following month in which he scored 49 in a run-chase of 84 against Pakistan, followed by an unbeaten 56 against Sri Lanka and 41 not out in the Final against Bangladesh in two more successful chases.

Kohli maintained his match-winning form in the 2016 ICC World Twenty20 in India, scoring 55 not out in another successful run-chase against Pakistan. He struck an unbeaten 82 from 51 balls in India's must-win group match against Australia in "an innings of sheer class" with "clean cricket shots". The knock helped India win by six wickets and register a spot in the semi-final; Kohli went on to rate the innings as his best in the format. In the semi-final, Kohli top-scored once again with an unbeaten 89 from 47 deliveries, but West Indies overhauled India's total of 192 and ended India's campaign. His total of 273 runs in five matches at an average of 136.50 earned him his second consecutive Man of the Tournament award at the World Twenty20. He was named as captain of the 'Team of the Tournament' for the 2016 World Twenty20 by the ICC.

Playing his first Test in the West Indies since his debut series, Kohli scored 200 in the first Test at Antigua to ensure an innings-and-92-run win for India, their biggest win ever outside of Asia. It was his first double hundred in first-class cricket and the first made away from home by an Indian captain in Tests.India went on to wrap the series 2–0 and briefly top the ICC Test Rankings before being displaced by Pakistan at the position. He scored another double hundred–211 at Indore in the third Test against New Zealand–as India's 3–0 whitewash victory saw them regain the top position in the ICC Test Rankings. In the subsequent ODI series, Kohli set up two wins for India batting second with unbeaten knocks of 85 at Dharamsala and 134-ball 154 at Mohali.He then made 65 in the series-deciding fifth game at Visakhapatnam which India won.

Kohli got double centuries in the next two Test series against England and Bangladesh, making him the first batsman ever to score double centuries in four consecutive series. He broke the record of Australian great Donald Bradman and fellow Indian Rahul Dravid, both of whom had managed to get three. Against England, he got his then-highest Test score of 235.

- *2017 ICC Champions Trophy*

Virat Kohli got the chance to captain in an ICC tournament for the first time in the 2017 ICC Champions Trophy. In the semi-final against Bangladesh, Kohli scored 96*, thus becoming the fastest batsman, in terms of innings, to reach 8,000 runs in ODIs in 175 innings.In the captaincy of Virat Kohli, the Indian cricket team reached the final, but lost to Pakistan by 180 runs. In the third over of Indian innings, Virat Kohli was dropped in the slips for just five runs but caught the next ball by Shadab Khan at point on the bowling of Mohammad Amir. He was also named as part of the 'Team of the Tournament' at the 2017 Champions Trophy by the ICC.

- *10,000 runs in ODIs before age of 30*

He followed it up with ODI centuries against the West Indies and Sri Lanka in consecutive series, equalling Ricky Ponting's tally of 30 ODI centuries. In October 2017, he was adjourned the ODI player of the series against New Zealand for scoring two ODI centuries, during the course of which he made a new record for the most runs (8,888), best average (55.55) and highest number of centuries (31) for any batsman when completing 200 ODIs. Kohli made several more records during the 3 match Test series against Sri Lanka at home in November.

After scoring a century and a double century in the first two Tests, he ended up scoring yet another double century in the third Test, during which he became the eleventh Indian batsman to surpass 5000 runs in Test cricket while scoring his 20th Test century and 6th double century. During this match he also became the first batsman to score six double hundreds as a captain.With 610 runs in the series, Kohli also became the highest run-scorer by an Indian in a three-match Test series and the fourth-highest overall. India comfortably won the three-match series 1–0 and Kohli was adjudged man of the match for the second and third Test matches and player of the series. With this win, India equalled Australia for the record streak of nine consecutive series wins in Test cricket. He ended the year with 2818 international runs, which is recorded as the third-highest tally ever in a calendar year and the highest tally ever by an Indian player. The ICC named Kohli as captain of both their World Test XI and ODI XI for 2017.

- *Overseas season-including Windies at home*

- Kohli fielding in a Test match against England at Trent Bridge in 2018

Kohli fared average in the Test matches as India lost 1–2 during the South Africa tour in 2018, but came back strongly to score 558 runs in the 6 ODIs, making a record for the highest runs scored in a bilateral ODI series. This included three centuries, remaining unbeaten in two with a best of 160*. India won the ODI series 5–1, Kohli becoming the first Indian captain to win an ODI series in South Africa.

In March 2018, Kohli decided to play county cricket in England in June, in order to improve his batting before the start of India's tour to England the following month.He signed to play for Surrey, but a neck injury ruled him out of his stint in England before it even began.On 2 August, Kohli scored his first Test century on English soil in the first test match of the series against England. On 5 August, Kohli displaced Steve Smith to become the No. 1 ranked Test batsman in the ICC Test rankings. He also became the seventh Indian batsman and first since Sachin Tendulkar in June 2011 to achieve this feat. In the third test at Trent Bridge, Nottingham, Kohli scored 97 and 103, and helped India win by 203 runs. At the end of 5-match test series, Kohli scored 593 runs, which was third highest runs by an Indian batsman in a losing test series. Kohli's consistent performance in the series against the moving ball when other batsman failed to perform was hailed by British Media as one of his finest. The Guardian describes Kohli's batting display as One of the Greatest batting display in a losing cause.

During ODI series against West Indies in 2018, Kohli became the 12th batsman and fastest player to score 10,000 ODI runs. He surpassed the milestone with 205 innings which is 54 innings less than the next quickest to the landmark, Sachin Tendulkar. In the course he scored his 37th ODI century. Kohli's average after crossing 10,000 is 59.62, which is also the best average among the 10,000 club members. On 27 October, after scoring his 38th ODI century, Kohli became the first batsman for India, first captain and tenth overall, to score three successive centuries in ODIs.He ended up scoring 453 runs in 5 innings, at an average of 151.00, in the 5-match series and was the Player of the Series.

On 16 December 2018 in the 2018-2019 Border Gavaskar Trophy, Kohli scored his 25th test hundred in Perth. His knock of 123 was his 6th hundred in three tours to Australia making him the only Indian to score 6 test hundreds in Australia after Sachin Tendulkar. He also became the fastest Indian and second fastest overall (125 innings) to score 25 test hundreds, second only to Donald Bradman (68 innings) which was bettered by Steven Smith during 2019 Ashes (119 innings).

Despite the fact that the Pitch was not as quick and bouncy as The WACA due to its drop-in nature it was still a tricky pitch where fast bowlers were getting assistant. Kohli's knock was rated by several analysts and former cricketers as one of his finest against a quality Australian attack. Although he broke several records in the game, his innings proved to insufficient as India went down by 146 runs as Australia levelled the series with two tests remaining. He had scored 82 in the third test at MCG, in which India won. Overall. he had finished the series with 282 runs at an average of 40.By winning the test series in Australia, he had become the first Indian and also the first Asian skipper to win a test series in Australia. He was again named as captain of both the World Test XI and ODI XI for 2018 by the ICC.

- *2019 Cricket World Cup*

In April 2019, he was named the captain of India's squad for the 2019 Cricket World Cup. On 16 June 2019, in India's match against Pakistan, Kohli became the fastest batsman, in terms of innings, to score 11,000 runs in ODI cricket. He reached the landmark in his 222nd innings. Eleven days later, in the match against the West Indies, Kohli became the fastest cricketer, in terms of innings, to score 20,000 runs in international cricket, doing so in his 417th innings. Kohli scored five consecutive fifty plus score in the tournament. India lost the semi-final against New Zealand, in which Kohli was out for just a run.

In October 2019, Kohli captained India for the 50th time in Test cricket, in the second Test against South Africa. In the first innings of the match,

Kohli scored an unbeaten 254 runs, passing 7,000 runs in Tests in the process, and became the first batsman for India to score seven double centuries in Test cricket.In November 2019, during the day/night Test match against Bangladesh, Kohli became the fastest captain to score 5,000 runs in Test cricket, doing so in his 86th innings. In the same match, he also scored his 70th century in international cricket.

In November 2020, Kohli was nominated for the Sir Garfield Sobers Award for ICC Male Cricketer of the Decade, as well as Test, ODI and T20I player of the decade and won two(Male cricketer of the decade and ODI cricketer of the decade). Also in November, Kohli played in his 250th ODI match, in the second match against Australia.

- *Disastrous tour of New Zealand*

Main article: Indian cricket team in New Zealand in 2019–20

India toured to New Zealand from January to March 2020 to play 5-match T20 series along with a 3 and 2-match ODI and test series respectively. During the tour, Kohli badly struggled against the moving ball on tricky New Zealand pitches throughout the tour making the tour as his worst ever after the England tour in 2014. During the entire tour he only managed 218 across formats in 12 innings at an average of 19.81 with one half-century during first ODI. This was his lowest aggregate of runs in a tour where he played in all formats. India managed to win the T20I series 5–0, However Kohli-led side was badly hammered during the ODI and Test leg of the tour losing 3-0 and 2-0 respectively. This was also India's first whitewash under Kohli's captaincy.

- *India's tour of Australia and home series vs. England*

India travelled to Australia during November 2020 till January 2021 for a long tour. During the ODI Series, Kohli managed to score two half-centuries in three innings with a aggregate of 173 runs at an average of 57.67 despite this India lost the series 2–1. However, India bounced backed strongly and clinch the T20I series 2–1 with Kohli being the highest run scorer in the series for India (134 runs at 44.37). During the first test of the tour played as Day/night match at Adelaide, Kohli scored a fluent 74 before being run out due to a wrong call by his batting partner Ajinkya Rahane, However he only managed 4 runs in next innings where India scrambled to 36/9, their lowest ever score in Test cricket history.

After the 1st Test, Kohli left the tour on paternity leave as he was expecting the birth of his first child. He received mixed responses for his decision. Indian batting great Sunil Gavaskar along with Kapil Dev slammed Kohli for leaving the tour after the Indian team lost the 1st Test in Adelaide. Gavaskar slammed the double standard of BCCI for Kohli getting the paternity leave while T. Natarajan wasn't allowed for the same. Despite his absence India managed to clinch the test series 2–1 under the able leadership of stand-in captain Ajinkya Rahane. The Daily Telegraph described India's recovery as one of the great comebacks in cricket history.

The England tour of India begin with a long 4-match Test series. Kohli struggled to find his form through the series as he managed 172 runs across 4 Test matches at an average of 28.66 with 2 half-centuries and 2 ducks. This was also the first time Kohli got out for two ducks in a Test series after his disastrous tour of England in 2014.However, during the second test at Chepauk, Kohli scored a crucial 62 on a minefield of a pitch which English batting great Geoffrey Boycott described as a template to bat and score runs on a turning pitch.

Kohli got out for a duck again in the 1st T20I of a 5-match series. However, he found his form in the latter part of the series and ended the series as the highest run-scorer from both sides with 231 runs to his name and 3 half-centuries at an average of 115.50 as India clinched the series 3–2. Kohli was adjudged as the Man of the Series for his performances. During the second T20I, Kohli became the first ever batsman to complete 3,000 runs in the format.

In the 3-match ODI series, Kohli managed to score 129 runs in 3 innings with 2 half-centuries at a moderate average of 43.00 as India won the series 2–1. During the 2nd ODI, Kohli became the second batsman after Ricky Ponting to score 10,000 runs batting at number 3.

- *World Test Championship Final and deaccession of T20 & ODI captaincy*

In June 2021, India lost the 2021 ICC World Test Championship Final to New Zealand. This was Kohli's third defeat as captain in knockouts and finals of ICC tournaments. Virat Kohli scored 44 and 13 runs in the 1st and 2nd innings respectively.

In September 2021, Kohli was named as the captain of India's squad for the 2021 ICC Men's T20 World Cup. Later the same month, Kohli announced that he would step down as India's T20I captain following the tournament. India could not make it through the semi-finals, which was the first time in the past 9 years.

In December 2021, Kohli was replaced by Rohit Sharma as India's ODI captain. BCCI President Sourav Ganguly later explained the decision to drop Kohli as ODI captain by saying that the selectors did not feel right to have two white ball captains.

- *Indian Premier League*

- Virat as the captain of RCB at 2015 IPL Opening Ceremony

Kohli was bought by the Indian Premier League franchise Royal Challengers Bangalore for $30,000 on a youth contract. He was the captain of Royal challengers Bangalore for 8 seasons but could not win a trophy.

- Kohli had an poor 2008 season, with a total of 165 runs in 12 innings at an average of 15.00 and a strike rate of 105.09.He did slightly better in the second season in which he made a total of 246 runs at 22.36, striking at over 112, while his team made it as far as the final. In the 2010 season, Kohli was the third highest run-getter for his team with 307 runs, averaging 27.90 and improving his strike rate to 144.81.

Kohli was the second-highest run-getter of the season, only behind teammate Chris Gayle, and his team finished as runners-up. Kohli scored total 557 runs at an average of 46.41 and at the strike rate of over 121 including four fifties. In the 2012 IPL, he averaged 28 and scored 364 runs.

- During 2013 season, Kohli averaged 45.28 and hit a total of 634 runs at a strike rate of over 138 including six fifties and a top-score of 99 and finished as the season's third-highest run-scorer.

Bangalore finished seventh in the next season in which Kohli made 359 runs at 27.61. He found success with the bat in the 2015 IPL in which he led his team to the playoffs. He finished fifth on the season's leading run-getters list with 505 runs at an average of 45.90 and a strike rate of more than 130.

- At the 2016 IPL, the Royal Challengers finished runners-up and Kohli broke the record for most runs in an IPL season (of 733 runs) by scoring 973 runs in 16 matches at an average of 81.08, winning the Orange Cap as well as Most-valuable Player Award of Vivo IPL 2016. He scored four centuries in the tournament, having never scored one in the Twenty20 format before the start of the season, and also became the first player to reach the 4000-run milestone in the IPL.At the launch event of his biography, 'Driven: The Virat Kohli Story' in New Delhi, in October 2016, Kohli announced that RCB would be the IPL franchise that he would permanently play for.

Kohli missed the start of the 2017 season due to a shoulder injury. Moreover, RCB finished the tournament at the bottom of the table, with Kohli scoring the most runs for his team, with 308 from 10 matches.On the occasion of the 10 year anniversary of IPL, he was also named in the all-time Cricinfo IPL XI.

In the 2018 season, Kohli was retained by RCB for a price of 170 million (US$2.3 million), the highest for any player that year. Kohli scored 530 runs in the season and became the first batsman to score more than 500 runs in 5 different seasons. Moreover, RCB failed to qualify for Playoffs and finished sixth on the points table.

On 28 March 2019, Kohli became the second player to reach 5000 IPL runs after Suresh Raina. In the same season, Kohli surpassed Raina to become leading runs scorer in IPL when he scored 84 runs in a match against KKR.

On 22 April 2021, against Rajasthan Royals, Kohli became the first ever player to reach 6000 IPL Runs. On 20 September, Royal Challengers Bangalore announced that Kohli would step down as captain following the 2021 IPL season.

- *Playing style*

- Kohli playing his famous flick shot in CWC 2015

Kohli is a naturally aggressive batsman with strong technical skills. He usually bats at the no.3 position in ODI cricket. He bats with a slightly open-chested stance and a strong bottom-hand grip. He is not a big hitter, so he can not hit big sixes and plays more grounded shots. He is known for his wide range of shots, ability to pace an innings and batting under pressure. He is strong through the mid-wicket and cover region. He has said that the cover drive is his favourite shot, while also saying that the flick shot comes naturally to him. He does not play the sweep shot often, being called "not a natural sweeper of the cricket ball". Kohli is strong on leg stump line bowling. If bowled at leg stump he plays flick shot.

According to cricket pundit VVS Laxman, for Virat Kohli, balling line outside the off stump is his weakness. He got out many times by outside off stump line ball and opposition team's bowlers tries to exploit his weakness in Test as well as ODIs Out swinging balls his one of the weakness as per Richard Hadlee.

His teammates have praised his confidence, commitment, focus and work ethics.Kohli is also known to be a "sharp" fielder.

Kohli is regarded as the best limited-overs batsman in the world, especially while chasing. In ODIs, he averages around 69 in matches batting second as opposed to around 51 batting first. 26 of his 43 ODI hundreds have come in run-chases and he holds the record for most hundreds batting second. Kohli is often compared to Sachin Tendulkar, due to their similar styles of batting, and sometimes referred to as Tendulkar's "successor". Many former cricketers expect Kohli to break Tendulkar's batting records. He is ranked as one of the world's most famous athletes by ESPN Kohli has stated that growing up his idol and role model was Tendulkar and that as a kid he "tried to copy the shots [Tendulkar] played and hit sixes the way he used to hit them."Former West Indies great Vivian Richards, who is regarded as the most destructive batsman in cricket, stated that Kohli reminds him of himself.In early 2015, Richards said Kohli was "already legendary" in the ODI format, while former Australian cricketer Dean Jones called Kohli the "new king of world cricket".

Kohli is noted for his on-field aggression and was described in the media as "brash" and "arrogant" during his early career. He has got into confrontations with players and umpires on several occasions. While many former cricketers have backed his aggressive attitude, some have criticised it. In 2012, Kohli had stated that he tries to limit his aggressive behaviour but "the build-up and the pressure or the special occasions make it tough to control the aggression."

- *Records*

Virat Kohli is leading run scorer in T20I with most 50 plus scores. He is the only cricketer to have been awarded player of the tournament twice in T20 World Cup. He scored 319 runs with 4 fifties in T20 World Cup 2014 and was leading run scorer in the tournament.

He has 2nd most centuries in ODI(43) and only behind Tendulkar who has 49 centuries. He has 3rd most centuries(70) in international cricket and only behind Tendulkar(100) and Ponting(71).He is the fastest player to score 10,000 runs in ODI in terms of innings and took 54 less innings than previous record of 259 innings. In 2018, He scored 1000 ODI runs in just 11 innings which is the least number of innings taken to score 1000 runs in a calendar year.

- Awards

1. Kohli receiving the Padma Shri award from President Pranab Mukherjee in March 2017
2. Kohli meeting Prime Minister of India Narendra Modi in New Delhi in 2017

- National honours

1. 2013 - Arjuna Award
2. 2017 - Padma Shri, India's fourth highest civilian award
3. 2018 - Rajiv Gandhi Khel Ratna award, India's highest sporting honour.

- Sporting honours

1. Sir Garfield Sobers Trophy (ICC Men's Cricketer of the Decade): 2011–2020
2. Sir Garfield Sobers Trophy (ICC Cricketer of the Year): 2017, 2018

- ICC ODI Player of the Year: 2012, 2017, 2018

1. ICC Test Player of the Year: 2018
2. ICC ODI Team of the Year: 2012,2014, 2016 (captain), 2017 (captain), 2018 (captain), 2019 (captain)
3. ICC Test Team of the Year: 2017 (captain), 2018 (captain), 2019 (captain)

4. ICC Spirit of Cricket: 2019
5. ICC Men's ODI Cricketer of the Decade: 2011–2020
6. ICC Men's Test Team of the Decade: 2011–2020 (captain)
7. ICC Men's ODI Team of the Decade: 2011–2020
8. ICC Men's T20I Team of the Decade: 2011–2020

- *Outside cricket*

- Personal life

Kohli with wife Anushka Sharma in their Mumbai reception
Kohli started dating Bollywood actress Anushka Sharma in 2013; the couple soon earned the celebrity couple nickname "Virushka". Their relationship attracted substantial media attention, with persistent rumours and speculations in the media, as neither of the two publicly talked about it. The couple married on 11 December 2017 in a private ceremony in Florence, Italy.On 11 January 2021, they became parents to a baby girl, Vamika.

In 2018, Kohli revealed that he completely stopped consuming meat to cut down his uric acid levels which caused him a cervical spine issue and started affecting his finger and, in turn, his batting. In 2021, he clarified that he is a vegetarian and not a vegan.

Kohli has admitted that he is superstitious. He used to wear black wristbands as a cricket superstition; earlier, he used to wear the same pair of gloves with which he had "been scoring". Apart from a religious black thread, he has also been wearing a kara on his right arm since 2012.

- *Commercial investments*

According to Kohli, football is his second favourite sport. In 2014, Kohli became a co-owner of Indian Super League club FC Goa. He stated that he invested in the club with the "keenness of football" and because he "wanted football to grow in India". He added, "It's a business venture for me for the future. Cricket's not going to last forever and I'm keeping all my options open after retirement."

In September 2015, Kohli became a co-owner of the International Premier Tennis League franchise UAE Royals and, in December that year, became a co-owner of the JSW-owned Bengaluru Yodhas franchise in Pro

Wrestling League.

In November 2014, Kohli and Anjana Reddy's Universal Sportsbiz (USPL) launched a youth fashion brand WROGN. The brand started to produce men's casual wear clothing in 2015 and has tied up with Myntra and Shopper's Stop. In late 2014, Kohli was announced as a shareholder and brand ambassador of the social networking venture 'Sport Convo' based in London.

In 2015, Kohli invested 900 million (US$12 million) to start a chain of gyms and fitness centres across the country. Launched under the name Chisel, the chain of gyms is jointly owned by Kohli, Chisel India and CSE (Cornerstone Sport and Entertainment), the agency which manages Kohli's commercial interests. In 2016, Kohli started Stepathlon Kids, a children fitness venture, in partnership with Stepathlon Lifestyle.

CHAPTER TWO

Let's Know About Cricket

- Cricket

Cricket is a bat-and-ball game played between two teams of eleven players on a field at the centre of which is a 22-yard (20-metre) pitch with a wicket at each end, each comprising two bails balanced on three stumps. The game proceeds when a player on the fielding team, called the bowler, "bowls" (propels) the ball from one end of the pitch towards the wicket at the other end. The batting side's players score runs by striking the bowled ball with a bat and running between the wickets, while the bowling side tries to prevent this by keeping the ball within the field and getting it to either wicket, and dismiss each batter (so they are "out"). Means of dismissal include being bowled, when the ball hits the stumps and dislodges the bails, and by the fielding side either catching a hit ball before it touches the ground, or hitting a wicket with the ball before a batter can cross the crease line in front of the wicket to complete a run. When ten batters have been dismissed, the innings ends and the teams swap roles. The game is adjudicated by two umpires, aided by a third umpire and match referee in international matches.

Forms of cricket range from Twenty20, with each team batting for a single innings of 20 overs and the game generally lasting three hours, to Test matches played over five days. Traditionally cricketers play in all-white kit, but in limited overs cricket they wear club or team colours. In addition to the basic kit, some players wear protective gear to prevent injury caused by the ball, which is a hard, solid spheroid made of compressed leather with a slightly raised sewn seam enclosing a cork core layered with tightly wound string.

The earliest reference to cricket is in South East England in the mid-16th century. It spread globally with the expansion of the British Empire, with the first international matches in the second half of the 19th century. The game's governing body is the International Cricket Council (ICC), which has over 100 members, twelve of which are full members who play Test matches. The game's rules, the Laws of Cricket, are maintained by Marylebone Cricket Club (MCC) in London. The sport is followed primarily in South Asia, Australasia, the United Kingdom, southern Africa and the West Indies.Women's cricket, which is organised and played separately, has also achieved international standard. The most successful side playing international cricket is Australia, which has won seven One Day International trophies, including five World Cups, more than any other country and has been the top-rated Test side more than any other country.

- History of cricket to 1725

A medieval "club ball" game involving an underhand bowl towards a batter. Ball catchers are shown positioning themselves to catch a ball. Detail from the Canticles of Holy Mary, 13th century.

Cricket is one of many games in the "club ball" sphere that basically involve hitting a ball with a hand-held implement; others include baseball (which shares many similarities with cricket, both belonging in the more specific bat-and-ball games category), golf, hockey, tennis, squash, badminton and table tennis. In cricket's case, a key difference is the existence of a solid target structure, the wicket (originally, it is thought, a "wicket gate" through which sheep were herded), that the batter must defend. The cricket historian Harry Altham identified three "groups" of "club ball" games: the "hockey group", in which the ball is driven to and fro between two targets (the goals); the "golf group", in which the ball is driven towards an undefended target (the hole); and the "cricket group", in which "the ball is aimed at a mark (the wicket) and driven away from it".

It is generally believed that cricket originated as a children's game in the south-eastern counties of England, sometime during the medieval period.Although there are claims for prior dates, the earliest definite reference to cricket being played comes from evidence given at a court case in Guildford in January 1597 (Old Style), equating to January 1598 in the modern calendar. The case concerned ownership of a certain plot of land and the court heard the testimony of a 59-year-old coroner, John Derrick, who gave witness that.

Being a scholler in the ffree schoole of Guldeford hee and diverse of his fellows did runne and play there at creckett and other plaies.

Given Derrick's age, it was about half a century earlier when he was at school and so it is certain that cricket was being played c. 1550 by boys in Surrey. The view that it was originally a children's game is reinforced by Randle Cotgrave's 1611 English-French dictionary in which he defined the noun "crosse" as "the crooked staff wherewith boys play at cricket" and the verb form "crosser" as "to play at cricket".

One possible source for the sport's name is the Old English word "cryce" (or "cricc") meaning a crutch or staff. In Samuel Johnson's Dictionary, he derived cricket from "cryce, Saxon, a stick". In Old French, the word "criquet" seems to have meant a kind of club or stick. Given the strong medieval trade connections between south-east England and the County of Flanders when the latter belonged to the Duchy of Burgundy, the name may have been derived from the Middle Dutch (in use in Flanders at the time) "krick"(-e), meaning a stick (crook). Another possible source is the Middle Dutch word "krickstoel", meaning a long low stool used for kneeling in church and which resembled the long low wicket with two stumps used in early cricket. According to Heiner Gillmeister, a European language expert of Bonn University, "cricket" derives from the Middle Dutch phrase for hockey, met de (krik ket)sen (i.e., "with the stick chase"). Gillmeister has suggested that not only the name but also the sport itself may be of Flemish origin.

- Growth of amateur and professional cricket in England

Evolution of the cricket bat. The original "hockey stick" (left) evolved into the straight bat from c. 1760 when pitched delivery bowling began.

Although the main object of the game has always been to score the most runs, the early form of cricket differed from the modern game in certain key technical aspects; the North American variant of cricket known as wicket retained many of these aspects. The ball was bowled underarm by the bowler and along the ground towards a batter armed with a bat that in shape resembled a hockey stick; the batter defended a low, two-stump wicket; and runs were called notches because the scorers recorded them by notching tally sticks.

In 1611, the year Cotgrave's dictionary was published, ecclesiastical court records at Sidlesham in Sussex state that two parishioners, Bartholomew Wyatt and Richard Latter, failed to attend church on Easter Sunday because they were playing cricket. They were fined 12d each and ordered to do penance.This is the earliest mention of adult participation in cricket and it was around the same time that the earliest known organised inter-parish or village match was played – at Chevening, Kent. In 1624, a player called Jasper Vinall died after he was accidentally struck on the head during a match between two parish teams in Sussex.

Cricket remained a low-key local pursuit for much of the 17th century. It is known, through numerous references found in the records of ecclesiastical court cases, to have been proscribed at times by the Puritans before and during the Commonwealth. The problem was nearly always the issue of Sunday play as the Puritans considered cricket to be "profane" if played on the Sabbath, especially if large crowds or gambling were involved.

According to the social historian Derek Birley, there was a "great upsurge of sport after the Restoration" in 1660. Gambling on sport became a problem significant enough for Parliament to pass the 1664 Gambling Act, limiting stakes to £100 which was, in any case, a colossal sum exceeding the annual income of 99% of the population. Along with prizefighting, horse racing and blood sports, cricket was perceived to be a gambling sport.Rich patrons made matches for high stakes, forming teams in which they engaged the first professional players.By the end of the century, cricket had developed into a major sport that was spreading throughout England and was already being taken abroad by English mariners and colonisers – the earliest reference to cricket overseas is dated 1676. A 1697 newspaper report survives of "a great cricket match" played in Sussex "for fifty guineas apiece" – this is the earliest known contest that is generally considered a First Class match.

- The patrons, and other players from the social class known as the "gentry", began to classify themselves as "amateurs" to establish a clear distinction from the professionals, who were invariably members of the working class, even to the point of having separate changing and dining facilities. The gentry, including such high-ranking nobles as the Dukes of Richmond, exerted their honour code of noblesse oblige to claim rights of leadership in any sporting contests they took part in, especially as it was necessary for them to play alongside their "social inferiors" if they were to win their bets. In time, a perception took hold that the typical amateur who played in first-class cricket, until 1962 when amateurism was abolished, was someone with a public school education who had then gone to one of Cambridge or Oxford University – society insisted that such people were "officers and gentlemen" whose destiny was to provide leadership. In a purely financial sense, the cricketing amateur would theoretically claim expenses for playing while his professional counterpart played under contract and was paid a wage or match fee; in practice, many amateurs claimed more than actual expenditure and the derisive term "shamateur" was coined to describe the practice.

- The Young Cricketer, 1768

The game underwent major development in the 18th century to become England's national sport.Its success was underwritten by the twin necessities of patronage and betting. Cricket was prominent in London as early as 1707 and, in the middle years of the century, large crowds flocked to matches on the Artillery Ground in Finsbury. The single wicket form of the sport attracted huge crowds and wagers to match, its popularity peaking in the 1748 season. Bowling underwent an evolution around 1760 when bowlers began to pitch the ball instead of rolling or skimming it towards the batter. This caused a revolution in bat design because, to deal with the bouncing ball, it was necessary to introduce the modern straight bat in place of the old "hockey stick" shape.

The Hambledon Club was founded in the 1760s and, for the next twenty years until the formation of Marylebone Cricket Club (MCC) and the opening of Lord's Old Ground in 1787, Hambledon was both the game's greatest club and its focal point. MCC quickly became the sport's premier club and the custodian of the Laws of Cricket. New Laws introduced in the latter part of the 18th century included the three stump wicket and leg before wicket (lbw).

The 19th century saw underarm bowling superseded by first roundarm and then overarm bowling. Both developments were controversial.Organisation of the game at county level led to the creation of the county clubs, starting with Sussex in 1839. In December 1889, the eight leading county clubs formed the official County Championship, which began in 1890.

The most famous player of the 19th century was W. G. Grace, who started his long and influential career in 1865. It was especially during the career of Grace that the distinction between amateurs and professionals became blurred by the existence of players like him who were nominally amateur but, in terms of their financial gain, de facto professional. Grace himself was said to have been paid more money for playing cricket than any professional.

The last two decades before the First World War have been called the "Golden Age of cricket". It is a nostalgic name prompted by the collective sense of loss resulting from the war, but the period did produce some great players and memorable matches, especially as organised competition at county and Test level developed.

- Cricket becomes an international sport

In 1844, the first-ever international match took place between the United States and Canada. In 1859, a team of English players went to North America on the first overseas tour. Meanwhile, the British Empire had been instrumental in spreading the game overseas and by the middle of the 19th century it had become well established in Australia, the Caribbean, India, Pakistan, New Zealand, North America and South Africa.

In 1862, an English team made the first tour of Australia. The first Australian team to travel overseas consisted of Aboriginal stockmen who toured England in 1868. The first One Day International match was played on 5 January 1971 between Australia and England at the Melbourne Cricket Ground.

In 1876–77, an England team took part in what was retrospectively recognised as the first-ever Test match at the Melbourne Cricket Ground against Australia. The rivalry between England and Australia gave birth to The Ashes in 1882, and this has remained Test cricket's most famous contest. Test cricket began to expand in 1888–89 when South Africa played England.

- World cricket in the 20th century

The inter-war years were dominated by Australia's Don Bradman, statistically the greatest Test batter of all time. Test cricket continued to expand during the 20th century with the addition of the West Indies (1928),

New Zealand (1930) and India (1932) before the Second World War and then Pakistan (1952), Sri Lanka (1982), Zimbabwe (1992), Bangladesh (2000), Ireland and Afghanistan (both 2018) in the post-war period. South Africa was banned from international cricket from 1970 to 1992 as part of the apartheid boycott.

• The rise of limited overs cricket

Cricket entered a new era in 1963 when English counties introduced the limited overs variant. As it was sure to produce a result, limited overs cricket was lucrative and the number of matches increased. The first Limited Overs International was played in 1971 and the governing International Cricket Council (ICC), seeing its potential, staged the first limited overs Cricket World Cup in 1975. In the 21st century, a new limited overs form, Twenty20, made an immediate impact. On 22 June 2017, Afghanistan and Ireland became the 11th and 12th ICC full members, enabling them to play Test cricket.

• A typical cricket field.

In cricket, the rules of the game are specified in a code called The Laws of Cricket (hereinafter called "the Laws") which has a global remit. There are 42 Laws (always written with a capital "L"). The earliest known version of the code was drafted in 1744 and, since 1788, it has been owned and maintained by its custodian, the Marylebone Cricket Club (MCC) in London.

• Playing area

Cricket is a bat-and-ball game played on a cricket field between two teams of eleven players each. The field is usually circular or oval in shape and the edge of the playing area is marked by a boundary, which may be a fence, part of the stands, a rope, a painted line or a combination of these; the boundary must if possible be marked along its entire length.

In the approximate centre of the field is a rectangular pitch (see image, below) on which a wooden target called a wicket is sited at each end; the wickets are placed 22 yards (20 m) apart. The pitch is a flat surface 10 feet (3.0 m) wide, with very short grass that tends to be worn away as the game progresses (cricket can also be played on artificial surfaces, notably matting). Each wicket is made of three wooden stumps topped by two bails.

- Cricket pitch and creases

As illustrated above, the pitch is marked at each end with four white painted lines: a bowling crease, a popping crease and two return creases. The three stumps are aligned centrally on the bowling crease, which is eight feet eight inches long. The popping crease is drawn four feet in front of the bowling crease and parallel to it; although it is drawn as a twelve-foot line (six feet either side of the wicket), it is, in fact, unlimited in length. The return creases are drawn at right angles to the popping crease so that they intersect the ends of the bowling crease; each return crease is drawn as an eight-foot line, so that it extends four feet behind the bowling crease, but is also, in fact, unlimited in length.

Before a match begins, the team captains (who are also players) toss a coin to decide which team will bat first and so take the first innings. Innings is the term used for each phase of play in the match.In each innings, one team bats, attempting to score runs, while the other team bowls and fields the ball, attempting to restrict the scoring and dismiss the batters. When the first innings ends, the teams change roles; there can be two to four innings depending upon the type of match. A match with four scheduled innings is played over three to five days; a match with two scheduled innings is usually completed in a single day. During an innings, all eleven members of the fielding team take the field, but usually only two members of the batting team are on the field at any given time. The exception to this is if a batter has any type of illness or injury restricting his or her ability to run, in this case the batter is allowed a runner who can run between the wickets when the batter hits a scoring run or runs,though this does not apply in international cricket. The order of batters is usually announced just before the match, but it can be varied.

The main objective of each team is to score more runs than their opponents but, in some forms of cricket, it is also necessary to dismiss all of the opposition batters in their final innings in order to win the match, which would otherwise be drawn. If the team batting last is all out having scored fewer runs than their opponents, they are said to have "lost by n runs" (where n is the difference between the aggregate number of runs scored by the teams). If the team that bats last scores enough runs to win, it is said to have "won by n wickets", where n is the number of wickets left to fall. For example, a team that passes its opponents' total having lost six wickets (i.e., six of their batters have been dismissed) have won the match "by four wickets".

In a two-innings-a-side match, one team's combined first and second innings total may be less than the other side's first innings total. The team with the greater score is then said to have "won by an innings and n runs", and does not need to bat again: n is the difference between the two teams' aggregate scores. If the team batting last is all out, and both sides have scored the same number of runs, then the match is a tie; this result is quite rare in matches of two innings a side with only 62 happening in first-class matches from the earliest known instance in 1741 until January 2017. In the traditional form of the game, if the time allotted for the match expires before either side can win, then the game is declared a draw.

If the match has only a single innings per side, then a maximum number of overs applies to each innings. Such a match is called a "limited overs" or "one-day" match, and the side scoring more runs wins regardless of the number of wickets lost, so that a draw cannot occur. In some cases, ties are broken by having each team bat for a one-over innings known as a Super Over; subsequent Super Overs may be played if the first Super Over ends in a tie. If this kind of match is temporarily interrupted by bad weather, then a complex mathematical formula, known as the Duckworth–Lewis–Stern method after its developers, is often used to recalculate a new target score. A one-day match can also be declared a "no-result" if fewer than a previously agreed number of overs have been bowled by either team, in circumstances that make normal resumption of play impossible; for example, wet weather.

In all forms of cricket, the umpires can abandon the match if bad light or rain makes it impossible to continue. There have been instances of entire matches, even Test matches scheduled to be played over five days, being lost to bad weather without a ball being bowled: for example, the third Test of the 1970/71 series in Australia.

• Innings

The innings (ending with 's' in both singular and plural form) is the term used for each phase of play during a match. Depending on the type of match being played, each team has either one or two innings. Sometimes all eleven members of the batting side take a turn to bat but, for various reasons, an innings can end before they have all done so. The innings terminates if the batting team is "all out", a term defined by the Laws: "at the fall of a wicket or the retirement of a batter, further balls remain to be bowled but no further batter is available to come in". In this situation, one of the batters has not been dismissed and is termed not out; this is because he has no partners left and there must always be two active batters while the innings is in progress.

- An innings may end early while there are still two not out batters

the batting team's captain may declare the innings closed even though some of his players have not had a turn to bat: this is a tactical decision by the captain, usually because he believes his team have scored sufficient runs and need time to dismiss the opposition in their innings

the set number of overs (i.e., in a limited overs match) have been bowled

the match has ended prematurely due to bad weather or running out of time

in the final innings of the match, the batting side has reached its target and won the game.

- Overs

The Laws state that, throughout an innings, "the ball shall be bowled from each end alternately in overs of 6 balls". The name "over" came about because the umpire calls "Over!" when six balls have been bowled. At this point, another bowler is deployed at the other end, and the fielding side changes ends while the batters do not. A bowler cannot bowl two successive overs, although a bowler can (and usually does) bowl alternate overs, from the same end, for several overs which are termed a "spell". The batters do not change ends at the end of the over, and so the one who was non-striker is now the striker and vice versa. The umpires also change positions so that the one who was at "square leg" now stands behind the wicket at the non-striker's end and vice versa.

- Clothing and equipment

English cricketer W. G. Grace "taking guard" in 1883. His pads and bat are very similar to those used today. The gloves have evolved somewhat. Many modern players use more defensive equipment than were available to Grace, most notably helmets and arm guards.

The wicket-keeper (a specialised fielder behind the batter) and the batters wear protective gear because of the hardness of the ball, which can be delivered at speeds of more than 145 kilometres per hour (90 mph) and presents a major health and safety concern. Protective clothing includes pads (designed to protect the knees and shins), batting gloves or wicket-keeper's gloves for the hands, a safety helmet for the head and a box for male players inside the trousers (to protect the crotch area). Some batters wear additional padding inside their shirts and trousers such as thigh pads, arm pads, rib protectors and shoulder pads. The only fielders allowed to wear protective gear are those in positions very close to the batter (i.e., if they are alongside or in front of him), but they cannot wear gloves or external leg guards.

Subject to certain variations, on-field clothing generally includes a collared shirt with short or long sleeves; long trousers; woolen pullover (if needed); cricket cap (for fielding) or a safety helmet; and spiked shoes or boots to increase traction. The kit is traditionally all white and this remains the case in Test and first-class cricket but, in limited overs cricket, team colours are worn instead.

- Bat and ball

Two types of cricket ball, both of the same size:

i) A used white ball. White balls are mainly used in limited overs cricket, especially in matches played at night, under floodlights (left).

ii) A used red ball. Red balls are used in Test cricket, first-class cricket and some other forms of cricket (right).

The essence of the sport is that a bowler delivers (i.e., bowls) the ball from his or her end of the pitch towards the batter who, armed with a bat, is "on strike" at the other end (see next sub-section: Basic gameplay).

The bat is made of wood, usually Salix alba (white willow), and has the shape of a blade topped by a cylindrical handle. The blade must not be more than 4.25 inches (10.8 cm) wide and the total length of the bat not more than 38 inches (97 cm). There is no standard for the weight, which is usually between 2 lb 7 oz and 3 lb (1.1 and 1.4 kg).

The ball is a hard leather-seamed spheroid, with a circumference of 9 inches (23 cm). The ball has a "seam": six rows of stitches attaching the leather shell of the ball to the string and cork interior. The seam on a new ball is prominent and helps the bowler propel it in a less predictable manner. During matches, the quality of the ball deteriorates to a point where it is no longer usable; during the course of this deterioration, its behaviour in flight will change and can influence the outcome of the match. Players will, therefore, attempt to modify the ball's behaviour by modifying its physical properties. Polishing the ball and wetting it with sweat or saliva is legal, even when the polishing is deliberately done on one side only to increase the ball's swing through the air, but the acts of rubbing other substances into the ball, scratching the surface or picking at the seam are illegal ball tampering.

- Player roles

Basic gameplay: bowler to batter
During normal play, thirteen players and two umpires are on the field. Two of the players are batters and the rest are all eleven members of the fielding team. The other nine players in the batting team are off the field in the pavilion. The image with overlay below shows what is happening when a ball is being bowled and which of the personnel are on or close to the pitch.

- Return crease

In the photo, the two batters (3 & 8; wearing yellow) have taken position at each end of the pitch (6). Three members of the fielding team (4, 10 & 11; wearing dark blue) are in shot. One of the two umpires (1; wearing white hat) is stationed behind the wicket (2) at the bowler's (4) end of the pitch. The bowler (4) is bowling the ball (5) from his end of the pitch to the batter at the other end who is called the "striker". The other batter (3) at the bowling end is called the "non-striker". The wicket-keeper (10), who is a specialist, is positioned behind the striker's wicket (9) and behind him stands one of the fielders in a position called "first slip" (11). While the bowler and the first slip are wearing conventional kit only, the two batters and the wicket-keeper are wearing protective gear including safety helmets, padded gloves and leg guards (pads).

While the umpire (1) in shot stands at the bowler's end of the pitch, his colleague stands in the outfield, usually in or near the fielding position called "square leg", so that he is in line with the popping crease (7) at the striker's end of the pitch. The bowling crease (not numbered) is the one on which the wicket is located between the return creases (12). The bowler (4) intends to hit the wicket (9) with the ball (5) or, at least, to prevent the striker (8) from scoring runs. The striker (8) intends, by using his bat, to defend his wicket and, if possible, to hit the ball away from the pitch in order to score runs.

Some players are skilled in both batting and bowling, or as either or these as well as wicket-keeping, so are termed all-rounders. Bowlers are classified according to their style, generally as fast bowlers, seam bowlers or spinners. Batters are classified according to whether they are right-handed or left-handed.

- Fielding

Of the eleven fielders, three are in shot in the image above. The other eight are elsewhere on the field, their positions determined on a tactical basis by the captain or the bowler. Fielders often change position between deliveries, again as directed by the captain or bowler.

If a fielder is injured or becomes ill during a match, a substitute is allowed to field instead of him, but the substitute cannot bowl or act as a captain, except in the case of concussion substitutes in international cricket. The substitute leaves the field when the injured player is fit to return. The Laws of Cricket were updated in 2017 to allow substitutes to act as wicket-keepers.

- Bowling and dismissal

Glenn McGrath of Australia holds the world record for most wickets in the Cricket World Cup.

Most bowlers are considered specialists in that they are selected for the team because of their skill as a bowler, although some are all-rounders and even specialist batters bowl occasionally. The specialists bowl several times during an innings but may not bowl two overs consecutively. If the captain wants a bowler to "change ends", another bowler must temporarily fill in so that the change is not immediate.

A bowler reaches his delivery stride by means of a "run-up" and an over is deemed to have begun when the bowler starts his run-up for the first delivery of that over, the ball then being "in play".

Fast bowlers, needing momentum, take a lengthy run up while bowlers with a slow delivery take no more than a couple of steps before bowling. The fastest bowlers can deliver the ball at a speed of over 145 kilometres per hour (90 mph) and they sometimes rely on sheer speed to try to defeat the batter, who is forced to react very quickly.

Other fast bowlers rely on a mixture of speed and guile by making the ball seam or swing (i.e. curve) in flight. This type of delivery can deceive a batter into miscuing his shot, for example, so that the ball just touches the edge of the bat and can then be "caught behind" by the wicket-keeper or a slip fielder. At the other end of the bowling scale is the spin bowler who bowls at a relatively slow pace and relies entirely on guile to deceive the batter. A spinner will often "buy his wicket" by "tossing one up" (in a slower, steeper parabolic path) to lure the batter into making a poor shot. The batter has to be very wary of such deliveries as they are often "flighted" or spun so that the ball will not behave quite as he expects and he could be "trapped" into getting himself out. In between the pacemen and the spinners are the medium paced seamers who rely on persistent accuracy to try to contain the rate of scoring and wear down the batter's concentration.

There are nine ways in which a batter can be dismissed: five relatively common and four extremely rare. The common forms of dismissal are bowled, caught, leg before wicket (lbw), run out and stumped. Rare methods are hit wicket,hit the ball twice, obstructing the field and timed out. The Laws state that the fielding team, usually the bowler in practice, must appeal for a dismissal before the umpire can give his decision. If the batter is out, the umpire raises a forefinger and says "Out!"; otherwise, he will shake his head and say "Not out".There is, effectively, a tenth method of dismissal, retired out, which is not an on-field dismissal as such but rather a retrospective one for which no fielder is credited.

- Batting, runs and extras

The directions in which a right-handed batter, facing down the page, intends to send the ball when playing various cricketing shots. The diagram for a left-handed batter is a mirror image of this one.

Batters take turns to bat via a batting order which is decided beforehand by the team captain and presented to the umpires, though the order remains flexible when the captain officially nominates the team. Substitute batters are generally not allowed, except in the case of concussion substitutes in international cricket.

In order to begin batting the batter first adopts a batting stance. Standardly, this involves adopting a slight crouch with the feet pointing across the front of the wicket, looking in the direction of the bowler, and holding the bat so it passes over the feet and so its tip can rest on the ground near to the toes of the back foot.

A skilled batter can use a wide array of "shots" or "strokes" in both defensive and attacking mode. The idea is to hit the ball to the best effect with the flat surface of the bat's blade. If the ball touches the side of the bat it is called an "edge". The batter does not have to play a shot and can allow the ball to go through to the wicketkeeper. Equally, he does not have to attempt a run when he hits the ball with his bat. Batters do not always seek to hit the ball as hard as possible, and a good player can score runs just by making a deft stroke with a turn of the wrists or by simply "blocking" the ball but directing it away from fielders so that he has time to take a run. A wide variety of shots are played, the batter's repertoire including strokes named according to the style of swing and the direction aimed: e.g., "cut", "drive", "hook", "pull".

The batter on strike (i.e. the "striker") must prevent the ball hitting the wicket, and try to score runs by hitting the ball with his bat so that he and his partner have time to run from one end of the pitch to the other before the fielding side can return the ball. To register a run, both runners must touch the ground behind the popping crease with either their bats or their bodies (the batters carry their bats as they run). Each completed run increments the score of both the team and the striker.

- Sachin Tendulkar is the only player to have scored one hundred international centuries

The decision to attempt a run is ideally made by the batter who has the better view of the ball's progress, and this is communicated by calling: usually "yes", "no" or "wait". More than one run can be scored from a single hit: hits worth one to three runs are common, but the size of the field is such that it is usually difficult to run four or more. To compensate for this, hits that reach the boundary of the field are automatically awarded four runs if the ball touches the ground en route to the boundary or six runs if the ball clears the boundary without touching the ground within the boundary. In these cases the batters do not need to run. Hits for five are unusual and generally rely on the help of "overthrows" by a fielder returning the ball. If an odd number of runs is scored by the striker, the two batters have changed ends, and the one who was non-striker is now the striker. Only the striker can score individual runs, but all runs are added to the team's total.

Additional runs can be gained by the batting team as extras (called "sundries" in Australia) due to errors made by the fielding side. This is achieved in four ways: no-ball, a penalty of one extra conceded by the bowler if he breaks the rules; wide, a penalty of one extra conceded by the bowler if he bowls so that the ball is out of the batter's reach bye, an extra awarded if the batter misses the ball and it goes past the wicket-keeper and gives the batters time to run in the conventional way leg bye, as for a bye except that the ball has hit the batter's body, though not his bat. If the bowler has conceded a no-ball or a wide, his team incurs an additional penalty because that ball (i.e., delivery) has to be bowled again and hence the batting side has the opportunity to score more runs from this extra ball.

- Specialist roles

Captain (cricket) and Wicket-keeper

The captain is often the most experienced player in the team, certainly the most tactically astute, and can possess any of the main skillsets as a batter, a bowler or a wicket-keeper. Within the Laws, the captain has certain responsibilities in terms of nominating his players to the umpires before the match and ensuring that his players conduct themselves "within the spirit and traditions of the game as well as within the Laws".

The wicket-keeper (sometimes called simply the "keeper") is a specialist fielder subject to various rules within the Laws about his equipment and demeanour. He is the only member of the fielding side who can effect a stumping and is the only one permitted to wear gloves and external leg guards. Depending on their primary skills, the other ten players in the team tend to be classified as specialist batters or specialist bowlers. Generally, a team will include five or six specialist batters and four or five specialist bowlers, plus the wicket-keeper.

- Umpires and scorers

Umpire (cricket), Scoring (cricket), and Cricket statistics
An umpire signals a decision to the scorers
The game on the field is regulated by the two umpires, one of whom stands behind the wicket at the bowler's end, the other in a position called "square leg" which is about 15–20 metres away from the batter on strike and in line with the popping crease on which he is taking guard. The umpires have several responsibilities including adjudication on whether a ball has been correctly bowled (i.e., not a no-ball or a wide); when a run is scored; whether a batter is out (the fielding side must first appeal to the umpire, usually with the phrase "How's that?" or "Owzat?"); when intervals start and end; and the suitability of the pitch, field and weather for playing the game. The umpires are authorised to interrupt or even abandon a match due to circumstances likely to endanger the players, such as a damp pitch or deterioration of the light.

Off the field in televised matches, there is usually a third umpire who can make decisions on certain incidents with the aid of video evidence. The third umpire is mandatory under the playing conditions for Test and Limited Overs International matches played between two ICC full member countries. These matches also have a match referee whose job is to ensure that play is within the Laws and the spirit of the game.

The match details, including runs and dismissals, are recorded by two official scorers, one representing each team. The scorers are directed by the hand signals of an umpire . For example, the umpire raises a forefinger to signal that the batter is out (has been dismissed); he raises both arms above his head if the batter has hit the ball for six runs. The scorers are required by the Laws to record all runs scored, wickets taken and overs bowled; in practice, they also note significant amounts of additional data relating to the game.

A match's statistics are summarised on a scorecard. Prior to the popularisation of scorecards, most scoring was done by men sitting on vantage points cuttings notches on tally sticks and runs were originally called notches.According to Rowland Bowen, the earliest known scorecard templates were introduced in 1776 by T. Pratt of Sevenoaks and soon came into general use.It is believed that scorecards were printed and sold at Lord's for the first time in 1846.

- thank you for buy & read this book

have a great day of your
from : Mr Vivek Kumar Pandey

www.ingramcontent.com/pod-product-compliance
Lightning Source LLC
Chambersburg PA
CBHW031432160726
47993CB00003B/1512